Early I for the Cello

by Cassia Harvey

CHP183

www.charveypublications.com - print books
www.learnstrings.com - PDF downloadable books
www.harveystringarrangements.com - chamber music

Finger Exercise 1

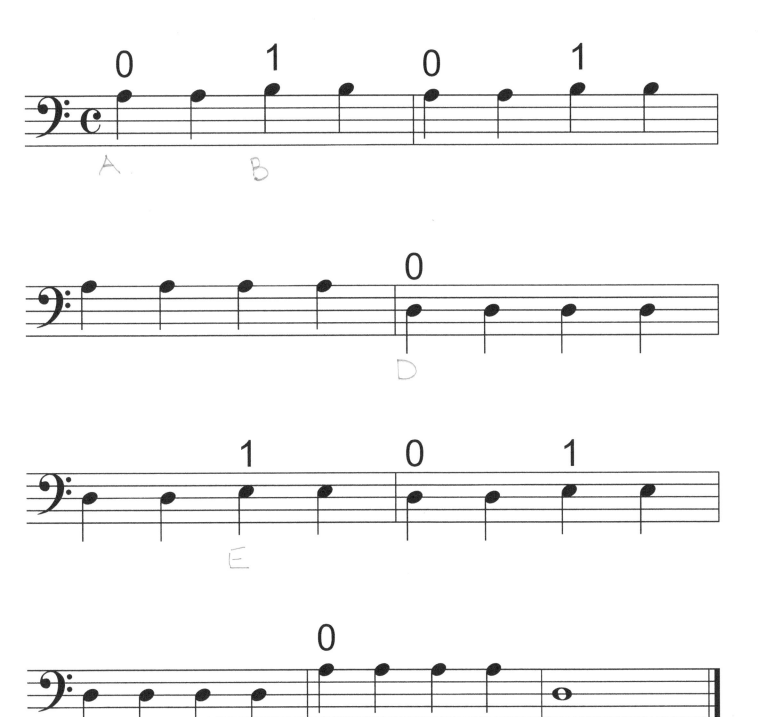

Rhythm 1
"Peanut-butter Sandwich"

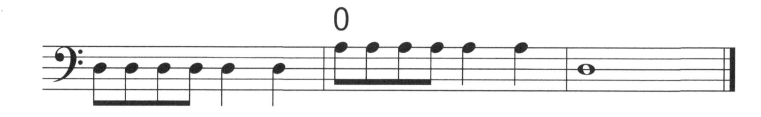

String Crossing 1

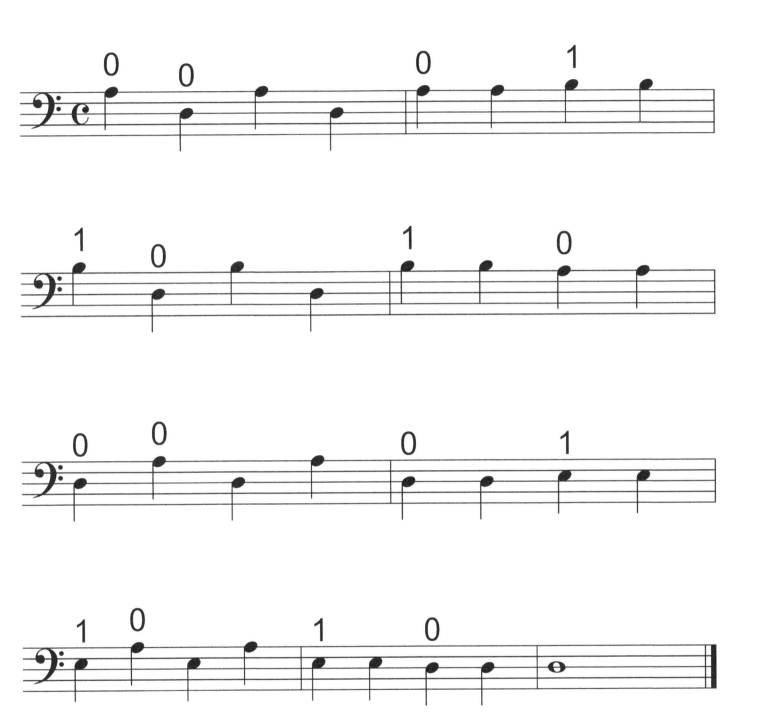

Finger Exercise 2

Rhythm 2
"Peanut-butter Sandwich"

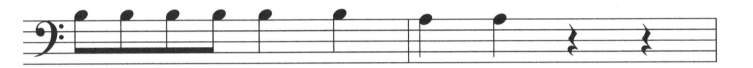

String Crossing 2

Finger Exercise 3

Rhythm 3
"Peanut-butter Sandwich"

String Crossing 3

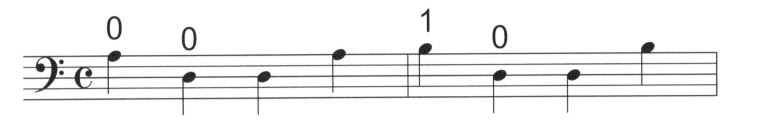

Finger Exercise 4

Rhythm 4
"Long-Short-Short"

String Crossing 4

Finger Exercise 5

Rhythm 5
"Long-Short-Short"

String Crossing 5

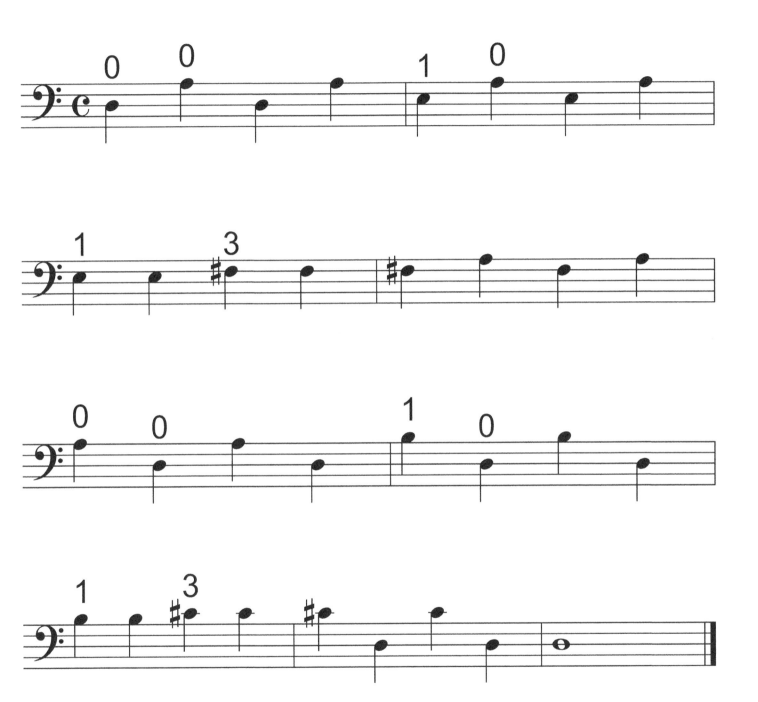

Finger Exercise 6

Rhythm 6
"Long-Short-Short"

String Crossing 6

Finger Exercise 7

Rhythm 7
"Short-Short-Long"

String Crossing 7

Finger Exercise 8

Rhythm 8
"Short-Short-Long"

String Crossing 8

Finger Exercise 9

Rhythm 9
"Short-Short-Long"

String Crossing 9

Finger Exercise 10

Rhythm 10
3 Beats in a Measure

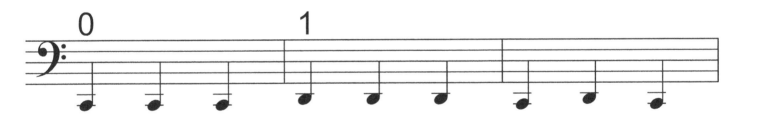

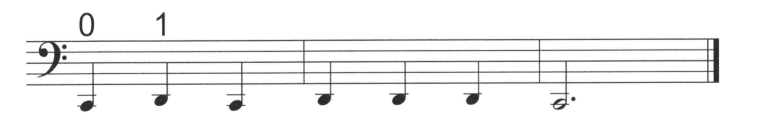

String Crossing 10: Slurs

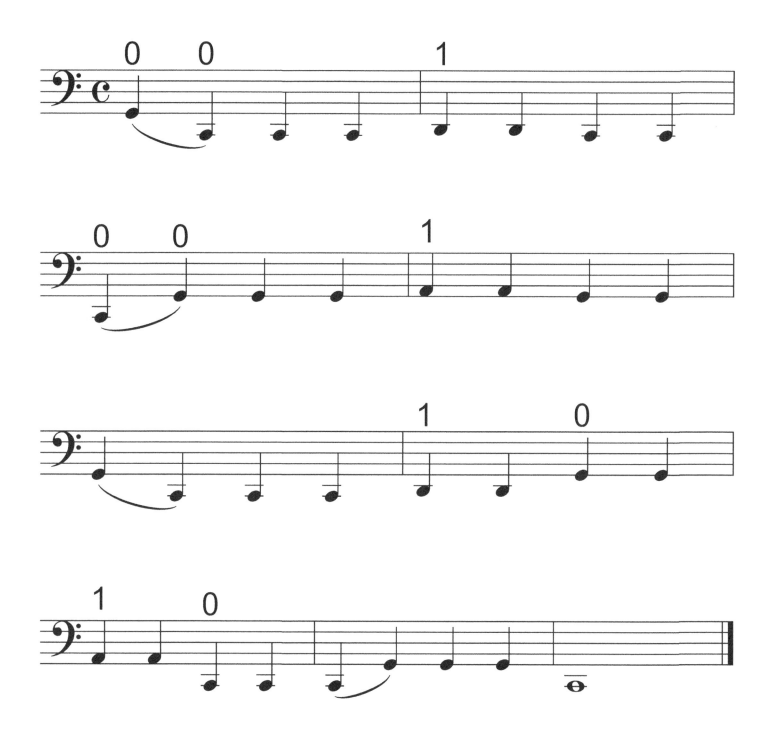

Finger Exercise 11

Rhythm 11
3 Beats in a Measure

String Crossing 11: Slurs

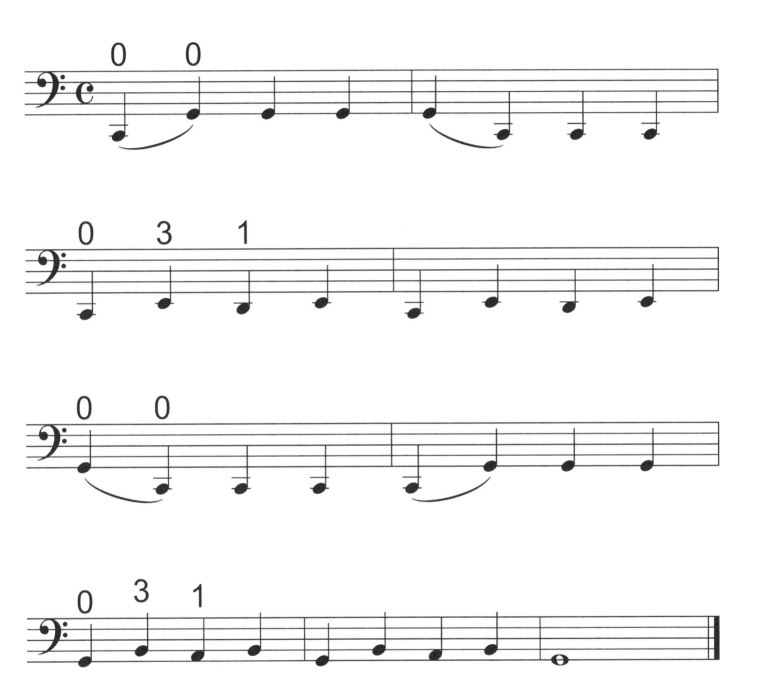

Finger Exercise 12

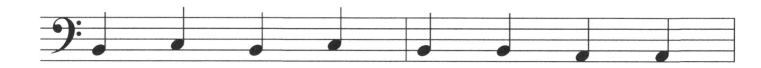

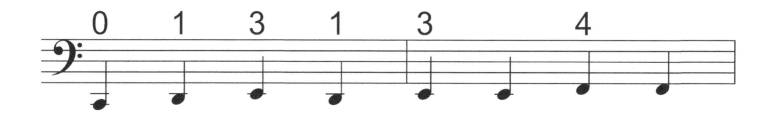

Rhythm 12
3 Beats in a Measure

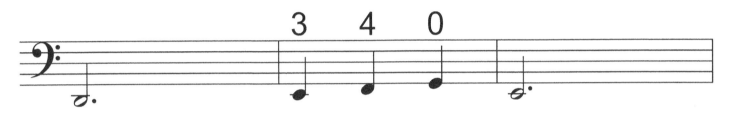

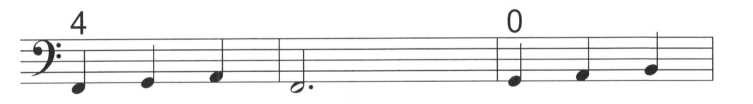

String Crossing 12: Slurs

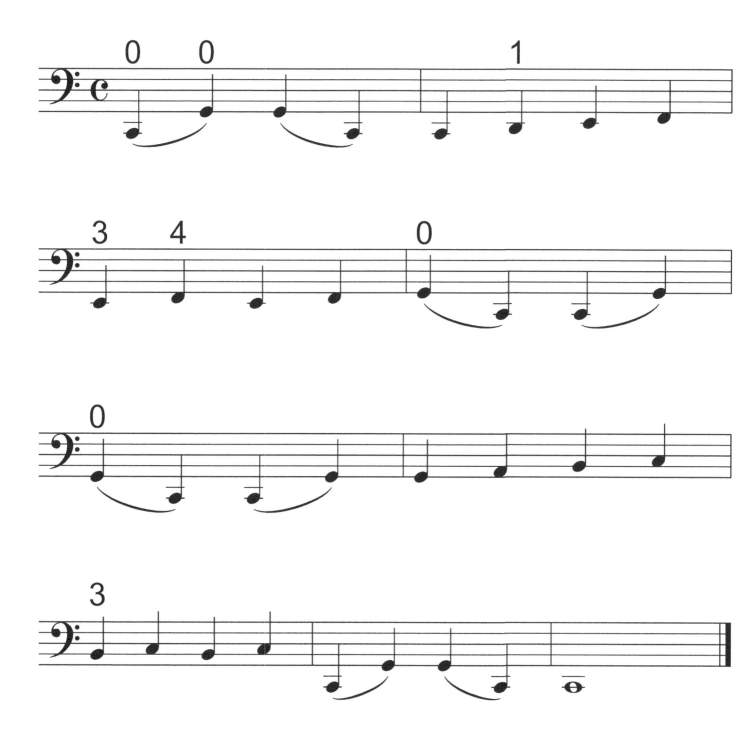

Finger Exercise 13

Rhythm 13
3 Beats in a Measure

String Crossing 13: Slurs

Finger Exercise 14: 2nd Finger

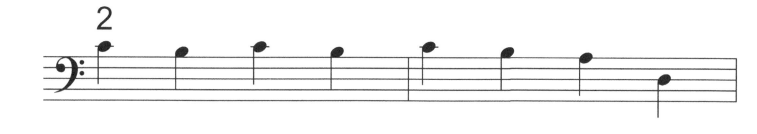

Rhythm 14
Half Note Rhythms

String Crossing 14: Slurs

Finger Exercise 15: 2nd Finger

Rhythm 15
Half Note Rhythms

String Crossing 15: Slurs

Finger Exercise 16: 2nd Finger

Rhythm 16
Half Note Rhythms

String Crossing 16: Slurs

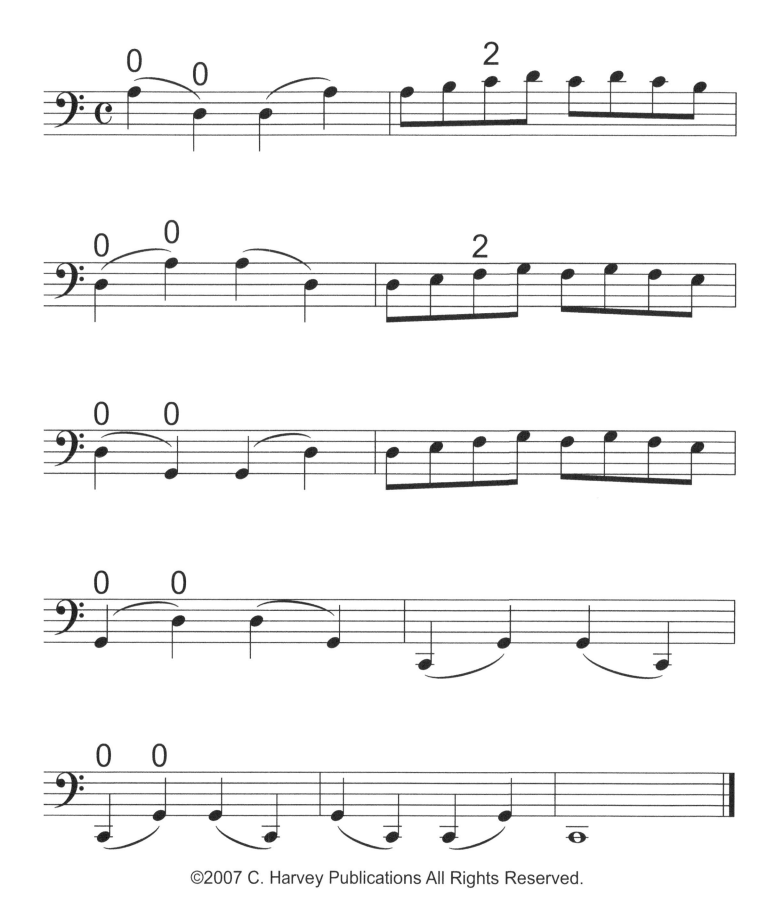

Beginning Fiddle Duets for Two Cellos

Cripple Creek

Trad., arr. Myanna Harvey

Made in the USA
Monee, IL
01 October 2021